FUN STUFF!

Finger Foods

Publications International, Ltd.

Pictured on the front cover (*clockwise from top left)*: Kids' Pizzas *(page 72)*, Strawberry Jam Sammies *(page 80)*, Chicken Corndog Bites *(page 88)* and Snake Snacks *(page 64)*.

Pictured on the back cover (*clockwise from top left):* Chicken Nuggets with Spicy Tomato Dipping Sauce *(page 18)*, Kitchen Sink Trail Mix *(page 34)*, Chocolate Chip S'More Bites *(page 92)* and Corn Dogs *(page 110)*.

ISBN: 978-1-4508-9564-4

Library of Congress Control Number: 2014948844

Manufactured in China.

8 7 6 5 4 3 2 1

Microwave Cooking: Microwave ovens vary in wattage. Use the cooking times as guidelines and check for doneness before adding more time.

Preparation/Cooking Times: Preparation times are based on the approximate amount of time required to assemble the recipe before cooking, baking, chilling or serving. These times include preparation steps such as measuring, chopping and mixing. The fact that some preparations and cooking can be done simultaneously is taken into account. Preparation of optional ingredients and serving suggestions is not included.

Contents

Dip Into It

Chocolate Peanut Butter Fondue

Makes 8 servings

⅓ cup sugar

⅓ cup unsweetened cocoa powder

⅓ cup milk

3 tablespoons corn syrup

2 tablespoons peanut butter

½ teaspoon vanilla

Assorted dippers: fresh fruit, pretzel rods and/or pound cake cubes

1. Combine sugar, cocoa, milk, corn syrup and peanut butter in medium saucepan over medium heat; cook and stir 5 to 7 minutes until heated through. Remove from heat; stir in vanilla.

2. Pour into medium bowl. Serve warm or at room temperature with assorted dippers.

Tip: Kids will enjoy eating fruit with this fondue!
Mix and match various types. Orange sections, pear slices
and fresh raspberries are just a few of the many kinds of fruit
you can serve with this sweet chocolate treat.

Peanut Butter 'n Yogurt Dip

Makes about 1 cup

Prep Time: 5 minutes

½ cup SKIPPY® Creamy or SUPER CHUNK®
  Peanut Butter
1 container (8 ounces) vanilla or fruit flavored
  yogurt

Suggested dippers: Sliced peaches, blueberries,
bananas or strawberries

1. Blend SKIPPY® Creamy Peanut Butter with yogurt in small bowl.

2. Serve with suggested dippers.

Bananas and Cheesecake Dipping Sauce

Makes 6 servings

½ cup sour cream
2 ounces cream cheese
2 tablespoons plus 1 teaspoon milk
2 tablespoons sugar

½ teaspoon vanilla
  Nutmeg
6 medium yellow or red bananas

Combine sour cream, cream cheese, milk, sugar and vanilla in blender; blend until smooth. Pour into small bowl; sprinkle with nutmeg. Serve immediately or cover and refrigerate until ready to serve. Serve with bananas.

Tropical Coconut Cream Dipping Sauce: Substitute coconut extract for vanilla.

Peanut Butter 'n Yogurt Dip

Ramen Hummus

Makes 2⅓ cups

1 package (3 ounces) chicken-flavored ramen noodles

1 can (15 ounces) chickpeas, rinsed and drained

¼ cup chopped fresh basil

1 medium clove garlic, minced

½ cup water

¼ cup extra virgin olive oil

3 tablespoons lemon juice

⅛ teaspoon ground red pepper

¼ teaspoon salt

Fresh bell pepper slices and pita chips

1. Prepare ramen noodles according to package directions, cooking on high heat 5 minutes instead of recommended 3 minutes. Rinse and drain under cold water to cool quickly.

2. Combine noodles, seasoning packet, chickpeas, basil, garlic, water, oil, lemon juice, ground red pepper and salt in food processor or blender; process until smooth, scraping down sides occasionally. Cover; refrigerate at least 1 hour before serving.

3. Serve with bell peppers and pita chips.

Zesty Fun Pretzel Dip

Makes 1 cup

Prep Time: 5 minutes

½ cup FRENCH'S® Spicy Brown Mustard

½ cup honey

Combine mustard and honey. Use for dipping pretzels, chips or cheese cubes.

Ramen
Hummus

Vanilla Almond Fruit Dip

Makes 2½ cups

2½ cups half-and-half
1 package (4-serving size) vanilla instant
    pudding mix (dry)
1 tablespoon sugar

1 teaspoon vanilla
1 teaspoon almond extract
    Fresh apple and peach slices, strawberries
    and/or bananas

Beat half-and-half, dry pudding mix, sugar, vanilla and almond extract in large bowl with electric mixer at medium speed 2 minutes. Serve immediately or refrigerate until ready to serve. Serve with fruit.

Easiest Three-Cheese Fondue

Makes 8 servings

2 cups (8 ounces) shredded mild or sharp
    Cheddar cheese
¾ cup milk
½ cup crumbled blue cheese
1 package (3 ounces) cream cheese, cut into
    cubes
¼ cup finely chopped onion

1 tablespoon all-purpose flour
1 tablespoon butter
2 cloves garlic, minced
4 to 6 drops hot pepper sauce
⅛ teaspoon ground red pepper
    Breadsticks and assorted fresh vegetables

Slow Cooker Directions

1. Combine Cheddar cheese, milk, blue cheese, cream cheese, onion, flour, butter, garlic, hot pepper sauce and ground red pepper in slow cooker. Cover; cook on LOW 2 to 2½ hours, stirring once or twice, until cheeses are melted and smooth.

2. Increase heat to HIGH. Cover; cook on HIGH 1 to 1½ hours or until heated through. Serve with breadsticks and fresh vegetables.

Vanilla Almond
Fruit Dip

Tamale Pie Dip

Makes about 5 cups

2 cups (8 ounces) shredded Mexican-style
   cheese, divided
1 package (8 ounces) cream cheese
1 can (8 ounces) creamed corn
1 can (8 ounces) diced tomatoes
½ cup sour cream
2 cloves garlic, minced

1 teaspoon chili powder
2 cups diced cooked chicken
1 teaspoon olive oil
   Optional toppings: Sour cream, chopped or
      sliced black olives, diced avocado, sliced
      green onions or diced tomato
Tortilla chips

1. Preheat oven to 325°F. Spray 9-inch quiche dish or deep-dish pie plate with nonstick cooking spray.

2. Combine 1 cup Mexican-style cheese, cream cheese, corn, tomatoes, sour cream, garlic and chili powder in food processor or blender; process until almost smooth. Stir in chicken. Spoon mixture into prepared dish. Top with remaining 1 cup Mexican-style cheese. Drizzle with oil.

3. Bake 45 minutes. Top as desired. Serve with tortilla chips.

Cheesy Mustard Dip

Makes 1¼ cups

Prep Time: 15 minutes

1 container (8 ounces) whipped cream cheese
¼ cup milk
3 tablespoons FRENCH'S® Spicy Brown Mustard
   or Honey Mustard

2 tablespoons mayonnaise
2 tablespoons minced green onions

Combine ingredients for dip in medium bowl; mix until well blended.

Tamale Pie Dip

Grilled Pineapple with Caramel Dipping Sauce

Makes 4 servings

25 **wrapped caramels**
⅓ **cup half-and-half**
¼ **teaspoon rum flavoring**

1 **ripe pineapple, trimmed and sliced**
   into 8 (½-inch) slices

1. Preheat grill over medium heat. Combine unwrapped caramels, half-and-half and rum flavoring in medium saucepan over low heat; cook and stir 3 to 5 minutes or until sauce is thickened and smooth. Keep warm.

2. Grill pineapple 10 to 12 minutes or until softened and deep yellow, turning halfway through grilling time.

3. Place pineapple on cutting board; cut into 1-inch pieces. Discard core pieces. Serve pineapple with caramel sauce.

Maple Mix Dip

Makes 4 to 6 servings

1 **box (4-serving size) cook and serve vanilla**
   pudding mix (dry)
2 **cups milk**
⅓ **cup maple syrup, divided**

¼ **teaspoon ground cinnamon**
   Assorted dippers: mini waffles, graham
   crackers, vanilla wafer cookies,
   apple slices and/or pear slices

1. Combine dry pudding mix, milk, 2 tablespoons maple syrup, and cinnamon in medium saucepan over medium heat; cook and stir 5 to 7 minutes or until thickened. Divide mixture evenly among four small bowls or custard cups.

2. Drizzle remaining syrup evenly over pudding surfaces. Allow cups to cool slightly before serving. Serve with assorted dippers.

**Grilled Pineapple
with Caramel
Dipping Sauce**

Quick and Easy Chocolate Fondue

Makes 12 servings

Prep Time: 5 minutes   **Cook Time:** 5 minutes   **Total Time:** 10 minutes

2 cups semi-sweet chocolate pieces
½ cup (1 stick) butter

Suggested dippers: PEPPERIDGE FARM® Cinnamon Swirl Bread, toasted and cut into strips; PEPPERIDGE FARM® Chessmen® Cookies; PEPPERIDGE FARM® Gingerman Homestyle Cookies; PEPPERIDGE FARM® Milano® Cookies

1. Cook and stir the chocolate and butter in an 8-inch heavy skillet over low heat for 5 minutes or until the chocolate is melted and smooth.

2. Pour the chocolate mixture into a fondue pot or a decorative bowl. Serve warm with the dippers.

Tip: You can also use this chocolate mixture to make festive chocolate and candy-coated puff pastry strips: Thaw **1** sheet PEPPERIDGE FARM® Puff Pastry. Unfold the pastry sheet on a lightly floured surface and roll into a 12-inch square. Cut into **72** (4×½-inch) strips and place onto baking sheets. Bake at 400°F. for 20 minutes or until golden brown. Dip the pastry strips in the warm chocolate mixture and sprinkle with crushed candy canes. Place on wax paper-lined baking sheets. Refrigerate or let stand at room temperature until chocolate is set.

Chicken Nuggets with Spicy Tomato Dipping Sauce

Makes 4 servings

Spicy Tomato Dipping Sauce (recipe follows)
½ cup panko bread crumbs
½ cup grated Parmesan cheese
1 package (3 ounces) ramen noodles, any flavor, finely crushed*
1 teaspoon garlic powder
1 teaspoon dried basil

½ teaspoon salt
¼ teaspoon black pepper
1 egg, lightly beaten
1½ pounds boneless skinless chicken breasts, cut into 1×2½-inch pieces
½ cup vegetable oil

Discard seasoning packet.

1. Prepare Spicy Tomato Dipping Sauce; set aside. Combine panko, cheese, noodles, garlic powder, basil, salt and pepper in large bowl. Place egg in shallow dish. Dip chicken in egg; shake off excess. Coat with panko mixture.

2. Heat oil in large skillet over medium heat. Add chicken in batches; cook 5 minutes or until cooked through. Serve with Spicy Tomato Dipping Sauce.

Spicy Tomato Dipping Sauce

Makes 1½ cups

1 tablespoon olive oil
1 small onion, chopped
2 cloves garlic, minced

¼ teaspoon ground red pepper
1 can (about 14 ounces) fire-roasted diced tomatoes

1. Heat oil in medium skillet. Add onion and garlic; cook and stir 3 minutes or until onion is tender and golden brown. Stir in ground red pepper.

2. Remove skillet from heat. Add skillet mixture and tomatoes to food processor or blender; blend until smooth. Return mixture to skillet over medium heat; cook 10 minutes or until thickened and reduced to 1½ cups.

Blue Cheese Dip for Pears

Makes about 1½ cups

Prep Time: 8 minutes   Chill Time: 1 to 2 hours

1 package (8 ounces) cream cheese, softened
⅓ cup KARO® Light or Dark Corn Syrup
2 teaspoons lemon juice

⅛ teaspoon ground ginger
½ cup (2 ounces) crumbled blue cheese
3 pears, thinly sliced

1. In small bowl with mixer at medium speed, beat cream cheese, corn syrup, lemon juice and ginger until smooth. Stir in blue cheese until mixed.

2. Cover; chill 1 to 2 hours.

3. Garnish with additional blue cheese crumbles. Serve with sliced fresh pears.

Peanut Butter S'Mores Dip

Makes 1 cup

Prep Time: 5 minutes

¼ cup SKIPPY® Creamy Peanut Butter
¼ cup skim milk
1 tablespoon unsweetened cocoa powder
1 cup frozen fat-free whipped topping, thawed

¼ cup mini marshmallows
6 plain or chocolate graham crackers, broken into individual crackers

Combine SKIPPY® Creamy Peanut Butter, milk, and cocoa powder in medium bowl. Fold in whipped topping, then marshmallows. Serve with graham crackers.

Tip: Make this treat more decadent by drizzling the plain graham crackers with melted bittersweet chocolate.

**Blue Cheese
Dip for Pears**

Peanutty Banana Dip

Makes 1 cup

½ **cup sliced bananas**
⅓ **cup creamy peanut butter**
2 **tablespoons milk**
1 **tablespoon honey**

½ **teaspoon vanilla**
⅛ **teaspoon ground cinnamon**
Sliced apples

Combine bananas, peanut butter, milk, honey, vanilla and cinnamon in blender; blend until smooth. Serve with apples.

Hot Beef 'n Cheddar Chili Dip with Fiesta Flats Scoops

Makes at least 24 servings

1 **pound ground beef**
1 **onion, diced (about 1 cup)**
1 **cup ORTEGA® Thick & Chunky Salsa, Medium**
1 **packet (1.25 ounces) ORTEGA® 40% Less Sodium Taco Seasoning Mix**

4 **cups shredded Cheddar cheese**
2 **boxes (12 shells each) ORTEGA® Fiesta Flats Flat Bottom Taco Shells**

BROWN ground beef and onion in large skillet over medium-high heat 6 to 8 minutes, stirring to break up meat. Drain fat.

ADD salsa, taco seasoning mix and ½ cup water. Stir until well combined.

REDUCE heat to low; add half of cheese. Stir until melted. Add remaining cheese. Cook and stir 4 minutes or until melted.

SERVE hot in heatproof bowl with the Fiesta Flats as dipping "scoops."

Peanutty
Banana Dip

Creamy Vegetable Dip

Makes 2 cups

Prep Time: 12 minutes plus refrigerating

- 2 packages (8 ounces each) cream cheese, softened
- ½ cup finely chopped broccoli
- ½ cup finely shredded carrot
- 2 tablespoons milk
- 2 tablespoons sliced green onion
- 1 tablespoon lemon juice
- 1 teaspoon grated lemon peel
- ½ teaspoon black pepper
- Assorted crackers

Beat cream cheese in medium bowl with electric mixer at medium speed 2 minutes or until smooth. Add broccoli, carrot, milk, green onion, lemon juice, lemon peel and pepper; mix 3 to 5 minutes or until well blended. Refrigerate until ready to serve. Serve with crackers.

Lemony Homemade Ranch Dip

Makes 2 cups

- ¾ cup buttermilk
- ½ cup mayonnaise
- ¼ cup sour cream
- 2 tablespoons grated lemon peel
- 1 tablespoon lemon juice
- 1 clove garlic
- 1 tablespoon fresh chives
- 1 tablespoon fresh basil
- 1 tablespoon fresh dill
- ½ teaspoon salt
- Assorted vegetable sticks

Combine buttermilk, mayonnaise, sour cream, lemon peel, lemon juice, garlic, chives, basil, dill and salt in food processor or blender; process until combined. Serve with vegetable sticks.

Creamy
Vegetable Dip

Chocolate Molé Fondue

Makes 6 servings

Prep Time: 15 minutes   **Start to Finish:** 25 minutes

CINNAMON CHIPS

2 tablespoons granulated sugar

2 teaspoons ground cinnamon

6 (8-inch) ORTEGA® Flour Soft Tortillas

Butter-flavored cooking spray

FONDUE

1 cup semisweet or dark chocolate chips

½ cup whipping cream

3 tablespoons ORTEGA® Taco Sauce, any variety

PREHEAT oven to 350°F. Combine sugar and cinnamon in small bowl. Set aside.

COAT one side of each tortilla with cooking spray. Cut into wedges; arrange in single layer on large baking sheet, coated side down. Sprinkle evenly with cinnamon-sugar. Spray again with cooking spray.

BAKE 8 to 10 minutes or until crisp, turning once.

COMBINE chocolate chips, whipping cream and taco sauce in small saucepan over low heat. Cook and stir until chocolate has melted and mixture is smooth.

KEEP chocolate mixture warm in small saucepan, slow cooker or fondue pot. Serve with cinnamon chips for dipping.

Pizza Fondue

Makes 20 to 25 servings

Prep Time: 15 minutes   Cook Time: 3 to 4 hours

½ pound bulk Italian sausage
1 cup chopped onion
2 jars (26 ounces each) meatless pasta sauce
4 ounces thinly sliced ham, finely chopped
1 package (3 ounces) sliced pepperoni, finely chopped

¼ teaspoon red pepper flakes
1 pound mozzarella cheese, cut into ¾-inch cubes
1 loaf Italian or French bread, cut into 1-inch cubes

Slow Cooker Directions

1. Brown sausage and onion in large skillet over medium-high heat 6 to 8 minutes, stirring to break up meat. Drain fat. Transfer sausage mixture to slow cooker.

2. Stir in pasta sauce, ham, pepperoni and red pepper flakes. Cover; cook on LOW 3 to 4 hours.

3. Serve with cheese and bread cubes.

Italian Dipping Sauce

Makes 8 servings

Prep Time: 5 minutes   Cook Time: 5 minutes   Total Time: 10 minutes

1 cup PREGO® Traditional Italian Sauce or Tomato, Basil & Garlic Italian Sauce

2 tablespoons grated Parmesan cheese
Assorted fresh vegetables for dipping

Heat the sauce and cheese in a 1-quart saucepan over medium heat until the mixture is hot and bubbling. Serve with the vegetables.

Pizza Fondue

BLT Dip

Makes 3 cups

Prep Time: 10 minutes

1 envelope LIPTON® RECIPE SECRETS® Onion Soup Mix*

1 cup HELLMANN'S® or BEST FOODS® Real Mayonnaise

1 container (8 ounces) sour cream

1 medium tomato, chopped (about 1 cup)

4 slices bacon, crisp-cooked and crumbled (about ⅓ cup)

Shredded lettuce (optional)

Also terrific with LIPTON® RECIPE SECRETS® Golden Onion Soup Mix.

1. Combine all ingredients except lettuce in medium bowl; chill, if desired.

2. Garnish with lettuce and serve with your favorite dippers.

Creamy Fiesta Dip

Makes about 5 cups

2 containers (16 ounces each) sour cream

½ cup chopped fresh chives

2 teaspoons onion powder

1 teaspoon minced garlic

1 teaspoon salt

1 cup shredded lettuce

1 tomato, chopped

1 can (about 2 ounces) sliced pitted black olives, drained

¼ cup chopped red onion

1 can (about 4 ounces) diced mild green chiles, drained

1 cup (about 4 ounces) shredded Cheddar cheese

Tortilla chips

1. Combine sour cream, chives, onion powder, garlic and salt in medium bowl; mix well. Spread in 13×9-inch baking dish.

2. Layer lettuce, tomato, olives, red onion, chiles and cheese over sour cream mixture. Serve with tortilla chips.

BLT Dip

Warm Peanut-Caramel Dip

Makes 1¾ cups

¼ cup peanut butter
2 tablespoons milk
2 tablespoons caramel ice cream topping

1 large apple, thinly sliced (24 slices)
4 large pretzel rods, broken in half

1. Combine peanut butter, milk and caramel topping in small saucepan over low heat; cook and stir 3 to 5 minutes or until mixture is melted and smooth.

2. Serve with apple slices and pretzels.

Microwave Directions: Combine peanut butter, milk and caramel topping in small microwavable dish. Microwave on MEDIUM (50%) 1 minute; stir well. Microwave an additional minute or until mixture is melted and warm.

Cucumber-Dill Dip

Makes about 2 cups

Salt
1 cucumber, peeled, seeded and finely chopped
6 green onions, white parts only, chopped
1 cup plain yogurt

1 package (3 ounces) cream cheese
2 tablespoons fresh dill *or* 1 tablespoon dried dill weed
Sprigs fresh dill (optional)

1. Lightly salt cucumber in medium bowl; toss. Refrigerate 1 hour. Drain cucumber; dry on paper towels. Return cucumbers to medium bowl; add green onions.

2. Combine yogurt, cream cheese and dill in food processor or blender; process until smooth. Stir into cucumber mixture. Cover; refrigerate 1 hour. Garnish with fresh dill sprigs.

Warm Peanut-Caramel Dip

By the Handful

Kitchen Sink Trail Mix

Makes about 4½ cups

1 to 1¼ cups granola cereal
½ cup raisins
½ cup red and green mini candy-coated chocolate pieces*
⅓ cup shredded sweetened coconut
¼ cup slivered almonds, toasted**
¼ cup coarsely chopped pecans, toasted**
¼ cup roasted salted green or white pumpkin seeds
¼ cup peanut butter chips

¼ cup chopped dried apricots***
¼ cup coarsely chopped dried cranberries***
¼ cup white chocolate chips
1 teaspoon ground cinnamon
⅓ teaspoon ground cardamom

*Or, substitute multicolored candy-coated chocolate pieces.

**To toast nuts, spread in single layer in small heavy skillet. Cook over medium heat 1 to 2 minutes, stirring frequently, or until lightly browned. Remove from skillet immediately. Cool before using.

***Spray knife with nonstick cooking spray to prevent sticking when chopping.

Combine cereal, raisins, chocolate pieces, coconut, almonds, pecans, pumpkin seeds, peanut butter chips, apricots, cranberries, chocolate chips, cinnamon and cardamom in large bowl; mix well.

Garlic-Parmesan Popcorn

Makes 12 cups

1 tablespoon olive oil
1 clove garlic, finely minced
1 tablespoon butter-and-oil spread, melted
12 cups plain popped popcorn

⅓ cup finely grated Parmesan cheese
½ teaspoon dried basil
½ teaspoon dried oregano

Stir oil and garlic into spread in small bowl until well blended. Pour over popcorn in large bowl; toss to coat. Sprinkle with cheese, basil and oregano.

Note: One regular-size microwavable package of popcorn yields about 10 to 12 cups of popped popcorn.

Spicy Fruity Popcorn Mix

Makes about 8½ cups

4 cups lightly salted popped popcorn
2 cups corn cereal squares
1½ cups dried pineapple wedges
1 package (6 ounces) dried fruit bits

Butter-flavored cooking spray
2 tablespoons sugar
1 tablespoon ground cinnamon
1 cup yogurt-covered raisins

1. Preheat oven to 350°F. Combine popcorn, cereal, pineapple and fruit bits in large bowl; mix lightly. Transfer to 15×10-inch jelly-roll pan. Spray mixture generously with cooking spray.

2. Combine sugar and cinnamon in small bowl. Sprinkle half of sugar mixture over popcorn mixture; toss lightly to coat. Spray mixture again with additional cooking spray. Add remaining sugar mixture; mix lightly.

3. Bake 10 minutes, stirring halfway through baking time. Cool completely in pan on wire rack. Add raisins; mix lightly.

Garlic-Parmesan Popcorn

Merlin's Magic Mix

Makes about 8 cups

6 cups unbuttered popped popcorn, lightly salted
1 cup pretzel nuggets
1 cup slivered almonds, toasted* and lightly salted
¼ cup (½ stick) butter
¼ cup light corn syrup

¾ cup firmly packed light brown sugar
⅓ cup cinnamon red hot candies
1 cup mini candy-coated chocolate pieces
¾ cup sweetened dried cranberries

To toast almonds, spread in single layer in small heavy skillet. Cook over medium heat 1 to 2 minutes, stirring frequently, or until lightly browned. Remove from skillet immediately. Cool before using.

1. Preheat oven to 250°F. Lightly grease two 13×9-inch baking pans; set aside. Place popped popcorn in large bowl. Add pretzel nuggets and almonds; set aside.

2. Heat butter and corn syrup in medium saucepan over low heat; cook and stir until melted and smooth. Add brown sugar; cook and stir until sugar is melted and mixture comes to a boil. Boil 5 minutes, stirring frequently. Remove from heat.

3. Stir in cinnamon candies until melted. Stir into popcorn mixture with lightly greased spatula until evenly coated. Spread popcorn mixture in even layer in prepared pans.

4. Bake 10 to 15 minutes, stirring every 5 minutes with lightly greased spatula to separate chunks. Cool completely in pans on wire racks.

5. Combine popcorn mixture, candy pieces and cranberries in large bowl. Store in tightly covered container.

Drizzled Party Popcorn

Makes about 8 cups

8 cups popped popcorn
½ cup HERSHEY'S® Milk Chocolate Chips

2 teaspoons shortening (do not use butter, margarine, spread or oil), divided
½ cup REESE'S® Peanut Butter Chips

1. Line cookie sheet or jelly-roll pan with wax paper. Spread popcorn in thin layer on prepared pan.

2. Place milk chocolate chips and 1 teaspoon shortening in microwave-safe bowl. Microwave at MEDIUM (50%) 30 seconds; stir. If necessary, microwave at MEDIUM an additional 10 seconds at a time, stirring after each heating, until chips are melted and smooth when stirred. Drizzle over popcorn.

3. Place peanut butter chips and remaining 1 teaspoon shortening in separate microwave-safe bowl. Microwave at MEDIUM 30 seconds; stir. If necessary, microwave at MEDIUM an additional 10 seconds at a time, stirring after each heating, until chips are melted and smooth when stirred. Drizzle over popcorn.

4. Allow drizzle to set up at room temperature or refrigerate about 10 minutes or until firm. Break popcorn into pieces.

Notes: Popcorn is best eaten the same day as prepared, but it can be stored in an airtight container. Recipe amounts can be changed to match your personal preferences.

Toll House® Party Mix

Makes 8 servings

Prep Time: 15 minutes   **Cooking Time:** 2 minutes   **Cooling Time:** 30 minutes

2 cups toasted cereal squares
2 cups small pretzel twists
1 cup dry-roasted peanuts
1 cup (about 20) caramels, unwrapped and
    coarsely chopped

1²⁄₃ to 2 cups (11- to 12-ounce package) NESTLÉ®
    TOLL HOUSE® Semi-Sweet Chocolate,
    Milk Chocolate, Butterscotch Flavored or
    Premier White Morsels

COAT 13×9-inch baking pan with nonstick cooking spray.

COMBINE cereal, pretzels, peanuts and caramels in large bowl.

MICROWAVE morsels in medium, uncovered, microwave-safe bowl on MEDIUM-HIGH (70%) power for 1 minute; STIR. Morsels may retain some of their original shape. If necessary, microwave at additional 10- to 15-second intervals, stirring just until morsels are melted. Pour over cereal mixture; stir to coat evenly.

SPREAD mixture in prepared baking pan; cool for 30 to 45 minutes or until firm. Break into bite-size pieces. Store in airtight container.

Choco-Peanut Butter Popcorn

Makes 6 servings

⅓ cup semisweet chocolate chips
3 tablespoons natural creamy peanut butter
1 tablespoon butter

4 cups air-popped popcorn
½ cup powdered sugar

Microwave Directions

1. Microwave chocolate chips, peanut butter and butter in medium microwavable bowl on HIGH 30 seconds; stir. Microwave 30 seconds or until melted and smooth. Pour mixture over popcorn in large bowl, stirring until evenly coated. Transfer to 1-gallon resealable food storage bag.

2. Add powdered sugar to bag; seal bag and shake until well coated. Spread onto waxed paper to cool. Store leftovers in airtight container in refrigerator.

Sweet and Spicy Popcorn Clusters

Makes 6 servings

½ cup sugar
6 tablespoons (¾ stick) butter
4 teaspoons corn syrup

½ teaspoon salt
½ teaspoon ground red pepper
12 cups popped light butter-flavored microwave popcorn

1. Combine sugar, butter, corn syrup, salt and ground red pepper in large saucepan. Bring to a boil over medium heat; boil 3 minutes. Remove from heat.

2. Immediately stir in popcorn; toss to coat evenly.

3. Spread mixture in single layer on baking sheets. Let stand 1 hour to cool completely. Break into clusters. Store in airtight container.

**Choco-Peanut
Butter Popcorn**

Ramen Border Mix

Makes about 6 cups

2 packages (3 ounces each) beef-flavored ramen noodles, coarsely chopped*

3 cups corn cereal squares

2 ounces cheese snack crackers

1 cup mixed nuts

3 tablespoons extra virgin olive oil

2 tablespoons prepared mustard

1 tablespoon Worcestershire sauce

2 teaspoons chili powder

1/8 teaspoon ground red pepper (optional)

Discard 1 seasoning packet.

1. Preheat oven to 300°F.

2. Combine noodles, cereal, crackers and nuts in large bowl; set aside.

3. Whisk 1 seasoning packet with oil, mustard, Worcestershire sauce, chili powder and ground red pepper, if desired, in small bowl. Spoon over cereal mixture; toss gently, yet thoroughly to coat completely. Place mixture on large baking sheet in single layer. Bake 20 minutes or until mixture begins to brown, stirring halfway through baking.

4. Remove from oven; place on wire rack to cool completely. Store mixture in airtight container.

Goobers® Trail Mix

Makes 10 servings

Prep Time: 10 minutes   **Cooking Time:** 10 minutes

2 cups NESTLÉ® GOOBERS® Milk Chocolate-Covered Peanuts

2 cups small pretzel twists

2 cups miniature marshmallows

1 cup raisins

1 cup coarsely chopped dried apricots

1 cup coarsely chopped dried apples

COMBINE GOOBERS®, pretzels, marshmallows, raisins, apricots and apples in large bowl.

Ramen
Border Mix

Apples 'n Cinnamon Popcorn

Makes 6 servings

Prep Time: 5 minutes   **Start to Finish Time:** 10 minutes

1 package plain microwave popcorn
¼ cup (½ stick) butter, melted

1 packet CREAM OF WHEAT® Apples 'n Cinnamon Instant Hot Cereal, uncooked

Microwave popcorn as directed on package. Carefully open bag and pour popcorn into large bowl. Drizzle on butter and toss to coat evenly. Sprinkle CREAM OF WHEAT® over popcorn and toss to coat evenly.

Tip: For a fun treat, serve with slices of apple. And for additional variety, toss the popcorn with another CREAM OF WHEAT® flavor.

Chewy Fruity Popcorn

Makes 10 cups

Prep Time: 15 minutes   **Cook Time:** 5 minutes

1 bag (2.9 ounces) microwave 94% fat-free butter popcorn, cooked according to package directions
1 package (5 ounces) dried cherries
1 cup dried apricots, chopped

1 cup sugar
½ cup light corn syrup
¼ cup finely chopped pecans
3 tablespoons PROMISE® Buttery Spread
1 teaspoon baking soda

1. Combine popcorn with fruit in large bowl sprayed with no-stick cooking spray; set aside.

2. Combine sugar with corn syrup in 1-quart glass measuring cup or microwave-safe bowl. Microwave at HIGH 4 minutes or until very pale yellow. Stir in pecans with heat-resistant rubber spatula or wooden spoon. Microwave at HIGH 1 minute or until pale yellow. Stir in PROMISE® Buttery Spread and baking soda.

3. Quickly and carefully drizzle mixture over popcorn and fruit, then stir constantly with spatula sprayed with no-stick cooking spray until popcorn and fruit are coated. Cool completely before serving.

Apples 'n Cinnamon Popcorn

Crisp Oats Trail Mix

Makes 2½ cups

1 cup old-fashioned oats
½ cup unsalted shelled pumpkin seeds
½ cup dried sweetened cranberries
½ cup raisins

2 tablespoons maple syrup
1 teaspoon canola oil
½ teaspoon ground cinnamon
¼ teaspoon salt

1. Preheat oven to 325°F. Line large baking sheet with heavy-duty foil.

2. Combine oats, pumpkin seeds, cranberries, raisins, maple syrup, oil, cinnamon and salt in large bowl; mix well. Spread on prepared baking sheet.

3. Bake 20 minutes or until oats are lightly browned, stirring halfway through baking time. Cool completely on baking sheet. Store in airtight container.

Bear Bite Snack Mix

Makes 4 cups

2 teaspoons sugar
¾ teaspoon ground cinnamon
¼ teaspoon ground nutmeg
1½ cups sweetened corn or oat cereal squares

1 cup raisins
1 cup teddy bear-shaped cookies
½ cup dried fruit bits or chopped mixed dried fruit
Nonstick cooking spray

1. Preheat oven to 350°F. Combine sugar, cinnamon and nutmeg in small bowl; mix well.

2. Place cereal, raisins, cookies and dried fruit in jelly-roll pan. Generously spray with cooking spray. Sprinkle with half of sugar mixture; stir well. Spray again with cooking spray; sprinkle with remaining sugar mixture.

3. Bake 5 minutes; stir. Bake 5 minutes more; stir. Cool completely in pan on wire rack. Store in airtight container.

Crisp Oats
Trail Mix

Fudgy Marshmallow Popcorn

Makes about 4 quarts

3½ quarts popped popcorn
2 cups sugar
1 cup evaporated milk
¼ cup (½ stick) butter

1 cup (½ of 7-ounce jar) marshmallow creme
1 cup (6 ounces) semisweet chocolate chips
1 teaspoon vanilla

1. Place popcorn in large bowl; set aside. Spray large baking sheets with nonstick cooking spray or line with parchment paper.

2. Combine sugar, evaporated milk and butter in medium saucepan. Cook over medium heat until sugar is dissolved and mixture comes to a boil, stirring constantly. Boil 5 minutes. Remove from heat.

3. Stir marshmallow creme, chocolate chips and vanilla into saucepan until chocolate is melted and mixture is smooth.

4. Pour chocolate mixture over popcorn, stirring until completely coated. Spread in single layer on prepared baking sheets. Refrigerate until set.

Hint: Remove any unpopped kernels before measuring the popped popcorn.

Terrific Trail Mix

Makes about 7 cups

3 cups QUAKER® Oatmeal Squares Cereal
1½ cups QUAKER® Oats (quick or old fashioned, uncooked)
⅓ cup roasted salted soy nuts or dry-roasted peanuts

¼ cup honey
2 tablespoons vegetable oil
1 cup mixed dried fruit bits
½ cup mini candy-coated milk chocolate candies

1. Heat oven to 350°F. Spray 15×10-inch jelly-roll pan with nonstick cooking spray.

2. Combine cereal, oats and soy nuts in large bowl. Combine honey and oil in small bowl; mix well. Add to cereal mixture; mix well. Spread mixture in single layer on prepared baking sheet.

3. Bake 12 to 15 minutes, stirring three times during baking. Remove from oven; stir to loosen mix from pan. Cool completely in pan on wire rack. Stir in dried fruit and candy. Store tightly covered.

Raisinets® Cereal Snacking Mix

Makes 6 servings

Prep Time: 10 minutes

2 cups toasted whole grain oat cereal
½ cup dried cranberries
2 tablespoons granulated sugar
½ teaspoon ground cinnamon

1 tablespoon butter, melted
1 cup (6.5 ounces) NESTLÉ® RAISINETS® Milk Chocolate-Covered Raisins or GOOBERS® Milk Chocolate-Covered Peanuts

COMBINE cereal and cranberries in large, resealable plastic bag.

COMBINE sugar and cinnamon in small bowl.

POUR cinnamon-sugar mixture and butter over cereal mixture; seal bag. Shake well to combine. Add RAISINETS® or GOOBERS®; shake well.

Terrific
Trail Mix

Cinnamon Caramel Corn

Makes 4 servings

8 cups air-popped popcorn (about ⅓ cup kernels)
2 tablespoons honey

4 teaspoons butter
¼ teaspoon ground cinnamon

1. Preheat oven to 350°F. Spray 15×10-inch jelly-roll pan with nonstick cooking spray. Place popcorn in large bowl.

2. Combine honey, butter and cinnamon in small saucepan; cook and stir over low heat until butter is melted and mixture is smooth. Immediately pour over popcorn; toss to coat evenly. Pour onto prepared pan.

3. Bake 12 to 14 minutes or until coating is golden brown and appears crackled, stirring twice.

4. Cool popcorn on pan. (As popcorn cools, coating becomes crisp. If not crisp enough, or if popcorn softens upon standing, return to oven and heat 5 to 8 minutes.) Store in airtight container.

Cajun Popcorn: Preheat oven and prepare jelly-roll pan as directed above. Replace cinnamon with 1 teaspoon Cajun or Creole seasoning and add 1 extra teaspoon honey. Proceed with recipe as directed above.

Italian Popcorn: Spray 8 cups air-popped popcorn with butter-flavored cooking spray to coat. Sprinkle with 2 tablespoons grated Parmesan cheese, ½ teaspoon dried oregano and ⅛ teaspoon black pepper. Gently toss to coat. Bake as directed.

Popcorn Granola

Makes 8 servings

1 cup quick oats
6 cups air-popped popcorn
1 cup golden raisins
½ cup chopped mixed dried fruit
¼ cup sunflower kernels

2 tablespoons butter
2 tablespoons packed light brown sugar
1 tablespoon honey
¼ teaspoon ground cinnamon
¼ teaspoon ground nutmeg

1. Preheat oven to 350°F. Spread oats on ungreased baking sheet; bake 10 to 15 minutes or until lightly toasted, stirring occasionally.

2. Combine oats, popcorn, raisins, dried fruit and sunflower kernels in large bowl. Heat butter, brown sugar, honey, cinnamon and nutmeg in small saucepan over medium heat until butter is melted. Drizzle over popcorn mixture; toss to coat.

Snackin' Cinnamon Popcorn

Makes 4 servings

1 tablespoon packed brown sugar
1 teaspoon salt
1½ teaspoons cinnamon

8 cups hot air-popped popcorn
Butter-flavored cooking spray

1. Combine brown sugar, salt and cinnamon in small bowl; mix well.

2. Spread popcorn in 15×10-inch jelly-roll pan; spray with cooking spray. Sprinkle with cinnamon mixture. Serve immediately or store in airtight container at room temperature up to two days.

Popcorn
Granola

Cinnamon Trail Mix

Makes 8 servings

2 cups corn cereal squares

2 cups whole wheat cereal squares or whole wheat cereal squares with mini graham crackers

1½ cups oyster crackers

½ cup broken sesame snack sticks

2 tablespoons butter, melted

1 teaspoon ground cinnamon

¼ teaspoon ground nutmeg

½ cup fruit-flavored candy pieces

1. Preheat oven to 350°F. Spray 13×9-inch baking pan with nonstick cooking spray.

2. Place cereals, oyster crackers and sesame sticks in prepared pan; mix lightly. Combine butter, cinnamon and nutmeg in small bowl; mix well. Drizzle evenly over cereal mixture; toss to coat.

3. Bake 12 to 14 minutes or until golden brown, stirring halfway through baking time. Cool completely. Stir in candies.

Teddy Bear Party Mix

Makes about 7 cups

Prep Time: 5 minutes   **Cook Time:** 12 minutes

4 cups crisp cinnamon graham cereal

2 cups honey flavored teddy-shaped graham snacks

1 can (1½ ounces) potato sticks

3 tablespoons melted unsalted butter

2 tablespoons FRENCH'S® Worcestershire Sauce

1 tablespoon packed brown sugar

¼ teaspoon ground cinnamon

1 cup sweetened dried cranberries or raisins

½ cup chocolate, peanut butter or carob chips

1. Preheat oven to 350°F. Lightly spray jelly-roll pan with nonstick cooking spray. Combine cereal, graham snacks and potato sticks in large bowl.

2. Combine butter, Worcestershire, sugar and cinnamon in small bowl; toss with cereal mixture. Transfer to prepared pan. Bake 12 minutes. Cool completely.

3. Stir in dried cranberries and chips. Store in an airtight container.

Cinnamon
Trail Mix

Popcorn & Pretzel Sweet Snack Mix

Makes 11 cups

Prep Time: 10 minutes   **Cook Time:** 3 minutes

REYNOLDS® Parchment Paper
1 bag (2.9 ounces) microwave low-fat popcorn
2 cups mini pretzels
1 cup coarsely chopped roasted almonds

1 cup coarsely chopped sweetened dried cranberries
1 bag (12 ounces) white chocolate chips
1½ teaspoons ground cinnamon

LINE a 15½×10×1-inch baking pan or large tray with REYNOLDS® Parchment Paper; set aside.

POP popcorn according to package directions; shake bag so that un-popped kernels fall to the bottom.

POUR popcorn, pretzels, almonds and dried cranberries into a large bowl. Discard un-popped popcorn kernels.

MELT white chocolate chips following package directions. Stir in cinnamon until well blended; pour over popcorn mixture. Toss to evenly coat.

SPREAD mixture evenly in parchment-lined pan. Let stand at room temperature to harden, about 1 hour. Break apart large pieces. Store in airtight container.

Party Nibbles

Snake Snacks

Makes 2 servings

2 small ripe bananas
1 tablespoon lemon juice
10 to 12 medium strawberries, hulled

2 small strawberries, hulled
1 slice kiwi (optional)

1. Peel and cut bananas crosswise into ¼-inch slices. Place in medium bowl; toss gently with lemon juice.

2. Leave 2 medium strawberries whole; cut remaining medium strawberries crosswise into ¼-inch slices.

3. Place whole strawberries on serving plates for heads; alternate banana and strawberry slices behind heads to form snakes. Arrange small strawberries at ends of snakes.

4. Cut four small pieces of banana for eyes; arrange on snake heads. Use toothpick to place kiwi seed in center of each eye, if desired.

Tip: Try to choose strawberries that are about the same diameter as the banana so all the fruit slices that make up the snake will be close to the same width.

Pizza Fries

Makes 8 servings

Prep Time: 20 minutes   **Bake Time:** 5 minutes   **Total Time:** 25 minutes

1 bag (2 pounds) frozen French fries
1 cup **PREGO®** Traditional or any variety
PREGO® Italian Sauce

1½ cups shredded mozzarella cheese
(about 6 ounces)
Diced pepperoni (optional)

1. Prepare the fries according to the package directions. Remove them from the oven. Pour the Italian sauce over the fries.

2. Top with the cheese and pepperoni, if desired.

3. Bake for 5 minutes or until the cheese is melted.

Ham & Cheese Snacks

Makes 4 servings

Prep Time: 20 minutes   **Chill Time:** 30 minutes

8 thin slices ham (about 6 ounces total)
2 tablespoons honey mustard

8 thin slices Muenster cheese (about
4 ounces total)
Thin pretzel crisps or favorite crackers

1. Spread each ham slice with about ¾ teaspoon mustard. Top 1 slice ham with 1 slice cheese; top with second slice of ham and cheese to create two double ham and cheese stacks.

2. Starting with long side, roll up each ham and cheese stack jelly-roll style into spiral. Wrap tightly in plastic wrap; refrigerate 30 minutes or up to 24 hours.

3. Cut each ham and cheese roll into ½-inch slices. Serve on pretzel crisps.

Pizza Fries

Mr. Froggy

Makes 4 servings

1 avocado
 Salt and black pepper
 Juice of 1 lime

4 ounces deli ham or turkey
4 corn tortillas
 Grape tomatoes, sliced

1. Mash avocado in small bowl; season with salt and pepper. Stir in lime juice. Keep covered. Cut out four tongue shapes from one slice of ham. Tear remaining ham into 1-inch pieces.

2. Working with one tortilla at a time, microwave tortillas on HIGH 20 to 30 seconds to soften. Fold tortilla in half; cut long ovals for eyes being careful to leave bottom edge of eye intact. Spread avocado mixture over one half of tortilla; top with shredded ham. Fold over, leaving eyes sticking up.

3. Heat large nonstick skillet over medium-high heat. Cook tortillas 1 to 2 minutes per side until heated through and lightly browned. Place on serving plate and add ham tongues and tomato slices for eyes.

Mr. Froggy

Extra Crunchy Chicken Tenders

Makes 4 to 6 servings

2 cups corn flakes
1 cup pretzels
½ teaspoon garlic powder
⅛ teaspoon paprika
⅛ teaspoon dry mustard
1 cup all-purpose flour
1 teaspoon salt

½ teaspoon ground black pepper
3 eggs, lightly beaten
1 teaspoon soy sauce
1 pound chicken tenders
Nonstick cooking spray
Ketchup and/or honey mustard

1. Preheat oven to 350°F. Spray large baking sheet with nonstick cooking spray.

2. Combine corn flakes and pretzels in food processor; pulse until coarse crumbs form. Transfer crumbs to shallow dish; stir in garlic powder, paprika and dry mustard. Combine flour, salt and pepper in another shallow dish. Combine eggs and soy sauce in third shallow dish.

3. Dredge chicken tenders in flour mixture; shake off excess. Dip in egg mixture, letting excess drip back into dish. Coat in crumb mixture, pressing lightly to adhere.

4. Spray large skillet with cooking spray; heat over medium heat. Working in batches, brown chicken on both sides. Transfer to prepared baking sheet.

5. Bake 10 minutes or until golden brown. Serve with ketchup and/or honey mustard.

Kids' Pizzas

Makes 6 (5- to 6-inch) pizzas

3 cups all-purpose flour
2 packages (¼ ounce each) active dry yeast
1 teaspoon salt
1¼ cups warm water, divided
¼ cup extra virgin olive oil
3 egg whites
1 tablespoon honey
1 teaspoon cider vinegar

Toppings
1 can (about 14 ounces) pizza sauce
  Italian seasoning
1 package (about 3 ounces) sliced pepperoni
  Shredded mozzarella cheese

1. Preheat oven to 450°F. Line baking sheet or pizza pans with parchment paper.

2. Mix flour, yeast and salt in large bowl. Whisk 1 cup warm water, oil, egg whites, honey and vinegar in medium bowl. Beat wet ingredients into dry ingredients with electric mixer at low speed until combined. Add additional water by tablespoonfuls until batter is smooth and thick. Beat at medium-high speed 5 minutes, scraping bowl occasionally.

3. Transfer one sixth of dough to prepared baking sheet. Pat dough into 5- or 6-inch circle using dampened fingers or back of oiled spoon, making crust thicker around edge to hold toppings. Repeat with remaining dough.

4. Bake 8 to 12 minutes or until crusts are lightly browned.* Top crusts with pizza sauce, Italian seasoning, pepperoni and cheese. Bake 2 to 5 minutes or until cheese is melted.

*To freeze pizza crusts for later use, allow them to cool, wrap well and store in the freezer up to three months.

Pigs in a Blanket

Makes 8 servings

Prep Time: 10 minutes **Cook Time:** 12 minutes

REYNOLDS® Parchment Paper
1 package (8 ounces) refrigerated
    reduced-fat crescent rolls

1½ teaspoons dry barbecue seasoning blend
4 slices Cheddar cheese, cut in half
8 turkey franks

PREHEAT oven to 375°F. Line a cookie sheet with REYNOLDS® Parchment Paper.

SEPARATE dough into triangles on parchment paper. Sprinkle each triangle with barbecue seasoning. Place cheese on wide end of triangle, leaving ¼-inch of dough around cheese.

ROLL UP each turkey frank, starting with the wide end of triangle, rolling toward the point.

BAKE 12 to 15 minutes or until golden brown. Serve immediately.

Mini Cheese Burritos

Makes 4 servings

½ cup canned refried beans
4 (8-inch) flour tortillas

½ cup chunky salsa
4 (¾-ounce each) Cheddar cheese sticks

Microwave Directions

1. Spread beans over tortillas, leaving ½ inch border around edges. Spoon salsa over beans.

2. Place cheese stick on one side of each tortilla. Fold edge of tortilla over cheese stick; roll up. Place burritos, seam side down, in microwavable dish.

3. Microwave on HIGH 1 to 2 minutes or until cheese is melted. Let stand 1 to 2 minutes before serving.

Pigs in a
Blanket

Burger Bliss

Makes 2 dozen sandwich cookies

Buns

1 package (about 16 ounces) refrigerated sugar cookie dough

½ cup creamy peanut butter

⅓ cup all-purpose flour

¼ cup packed brown sugar

½ teaspoon vanilla

Beaten egg white and sesame seeds (optional)

Burgers

½ (16-ounce) package refrigerated sugar cookie dough*

3 tablespoons unsweetened cocoa powder

2 tablespoons packed brown sugar

½ teaspoon vanilla

Red, yellow and green decorating icings

Reserve remaining dough for another use.

1. Preheat oven to 350°F. Spray large cookie sheets with nonstick cooking spray.

2. For buns, let 1 package dough stand at room temperature 15 minutes. Combine 1 package dough, peanut butter, flour, ¼ cup brown sugar and ½ teaspoon vanilla in large bowl; beat with electric mixer at medium speed until well blended. Shape into 48 (1-inch) balls; place 2 inches apart on prepared cookie sheets.

3. Bake 14 minutes or until lightly browned. Brush half of cookies with egg white and sprinkle with sesame seeds after 10 minutes, if desired. Cool on cookie sheets 2 minutes. Remove to wire racks; cool completely.

4. For burgers, let ½ package dough stand at room temperature 15 minutes. Beat dough, cocoa, 2 tablespoons brown sugar and ½ teaspoon vanilla in medium bowl with electric mixer at medium speed until well blended. Shape into 24 (1-inch) balls; place 2 inches apart on prepared cookie sheets. Flatten to ¼-inch thickness.

5. Bake 12 minutes or until set. Cool on cookie sheets 2 minutes. Remove to wire racks; cool completely.

6. To assemble, use icing to attach burgers to flat side of 24 buns. Pipe red, yellow and green icings on burgers to resemble condiments. Top with remaining buns.

Twisty Sticks

Makes 2½ dozen

1 package (about 16 ounces) refrigerated
   sugar cookie dough
6 tablespoons all-purpose flour, divided
1 tablespoon unsweetened cocoa powder

2 tablespoons creamy peanut butter
1 cup semisweet chocolate chips
1 tablespoon shortening
   Colored sprinkles and finely chopped peanuts

1. Remove dough from wrapper. Divide dough in half; place in separate medium bowls. Let stand at room temperature about 15 minutes.

2. Add 3 tablespoons flour and cocoa to half of dough; beat with electric mixer at medium speed until well blended. Wrap in plastic wrap; refrigerate at least 1 hour.

3. Add remaining 3 tablespoons flour and peanut butter to remaining half of dough; beat with electric mixer at medium speed until well blended. Wrap in plastic wrap; refrigerate at least 1 hour.

4. Preheat oven to 350°F. Divide chocolate dough into 30 equal pieces. Divide peanut butter dough into 30 equal pieces. Shape each dough piece into 4-inch-long rope on lightly floured surface. For each cookie, twist 1 chocolate rope and 1 peanut butter rope together. Place 2 inches apart on ungreased cookie sheets. Bake 7 to 10 minutes or until set. Remove to wire racks to cool completely.

5. Meanwhile, combine chocolate chips and shortening in small microwavable bowl. Microwave on HIGH 1 minute; stir. Microwave on HIGH at additional 30-second intervals until chips and shortening are completely melted and smooth. Spread chocolate on one end of each cookie; top with sprinkles and peanuts as desired. Place on waxed paper. Let stand 30 minutes or until set.

Strawberry Jam Sammies

Makes about 12 servings

1 bag (16 ounces) frozen strawberries
  or mixed berries
½ cup sugar

Juice of ½ lemon
12 slices whole grain sandwich bread

Microwave Directions

1. Combine strawberries and sugar in 3-quart microwavable measuring cup or casserole dish. Microwave, uncovered, on HIGH 2 minutes; stir and cut large berries into small pieces.

2. Stir in lemon juice. Return to microwave and cook 10 minutes, stirring after 5 minutes. Watch closely and stir once or twice to prevent boiling over.

3. To test thickness of jam, put a spoonful on small saucer and place in freezer 1 minute. If you want thicker jam, microwave 2 to 4 additional minutes, stirring as necessary.

4. Allow jam to cool completely. Make sammies by cutting shapes from bread using assorted cookie cutters. Pour remaining jam into storage containers. Jam will keep in refrigerator up to two weeks or in freezer up to four months.

Marshmallow Snowmen

Makes 12 snowmen

Prep Time: 1 hour   **Cooking Time:** 10 minutes

12 squares NESTLÉ® TOLL HOUSE® Refrigerated Chocolate Chip Cookie Bar Dough

12 NESTLÉ® CRUNCH® or NESTLÉ® BUTTERFINGER® Jingles candy, unwrapped

12 pretzel checkerboard snaps or mini pretzels for hat base

⅔ cup prepared white frosting

24 large marshmallows, *divided*

12 pretzel sticks for arms, broken in half NESTLÉ® TOLL HOUSE® Semi-Sweet Chocolate Mini Morsels for eyes and buttons (a heaping teaspoon needed)

12 small orange candies or orange decorating gel for nose

Thin-string licorice, various colors, cut into twelve, 7-inch pieces for scarves

PREPARE 12 cookies as directed on package. Cool on baking sheet for 2 minutes; remove to wire rack to cool completely.

TO MAKE HATS, ADHERE Jingles to pretzel snaps with frosting. Set aside.

TO MAKE SNOWMEN, INSERT 2 pretzel sticks into each side of *12* marshmallows to create arms on base of snowman. Spread a heaping teaspoon of frosting onto center of each cookie; top with snowman base. Press down lightly. Spread additional frosting on top of each snowman base. Top with *remaining 12* marshmallows. Dip orange candies and mini morsels into frosting and add noses, eyes and buttons to snowmen. For scarf, tie each piece of licorice loosely around neck of snowman using frosting as glue, if necessary. Let both hats and snowmen bases stand for 20 minutes to set frosting and make snowmen stable.

PRIOR TO SERVING, adhere hats to snowman head with frosting. If snowmen need to set up more, lean them against a glass or can to set.

Sloppy Joe's Bun Buggy

Makes 4 servings

4 hot dog buns (not split)
16 thin slices cucumber or zucchini
24 matchstick-size carrot strips, 1 inch long
4 black olives or pimiento-stuffed olives
Nonstick cooking spray
1 (10-ounce) package ground turkey
1¼ cups prepared pasta sauce

½ cup chopped broccoli stems
2 teaspoons prepared mustard
½ teaspoon Worcestershire sauce
Dash salt
Dash black pepper
4 small pretzel twists

1. Hollow out hot dog buns. Use toothpick to make four holes in sides of each bun to attach "wheels." Use toothpick to make one hole in center of each cucumber slice; push carrot strip through hole. Press into holes in buns, making "wheels" on buns.

2. Cut each olive in half horizontally. Use toothpick to make two holes in one end of each bun to attach "headlights." Use carrot strips to attach olives to buns, making "headlights."

3. Spray large skillet with cooking spray. Add turkey; cook and stir over medium heat until no longer pink. Stir in pasta sauce, broccoli, mustard, Worcestershire sauce, salt and pepper; heat through.

4. Spoon turkey mixture into hollowed-out buns. Press pretzel twist into turkey mixture, making "windshield" on each buggy.

Mini Pickle Sea Monster Burgers

Makes 12 mini burgers

4 large hamburger buns, split
2 whole dill pickles
1 pound ground beef
2 tablespoons steak sauce

Salt and black pepper
3 slices American cheese,
   each cut into 4 squares
Ketchup

1. Preheat broiler. Spray broiler rack and pan with nonstick cooking spray.

2. Cut three circles out of each bun half with 2-inch biscuit cutter. (Discard scraps or use to make bread crumbs for another use.)

3. Cut pickles lengthwise into thin slices. Using 12 largest slices, cut 4 to 5 slits on one end of each slice, about ½ inch deep; fan slightly to resemble fish tails. Save remaining slices for another use.

4. Combine ground beef and steak sauce in medium bowl; mix just until blended. Shape meat into 12 (2½×¼-inch) patties. Place on broiler rack. Sprinkle with salt and pepper. Broil 4 inches from heat 2 minutes. Turn patties; broil 2 minutes or until no longer pink in center. Remove from heat; top with cheese squares.

5. Arrange bun bottoms on serving platter; top with ketchup and pickle slices, making sure slices stick out at both ends. Place cheeseburgers on top of pickles; top with bun tops. Place drop of ketchup on uncut end of pickles for eyes.

Note: To save time, look for mini buns at the supermarket in place of cutting the hamburger buns.

Chicken Corndog Bites

Makes 16 bites

1 package (11½ ounces) refrigerated corn
    breadstick dough (8 count)
1 package (10 ounces) Italian-seasoned chicken
    breast strips, cooked

Mustard
Ketchup

1. Preheat oven to 375°F. Line baking sheet with parchment paper or foil.

2. Unroll dough, separate into individual breadsticks. Roll out each breadstick to 7×1½-inch rectangle (¼ inch thick). Cut each piece of dough in half crosswise to form 16 pieces total.

3. Cut chicken strips in half crosswise. Place one piece of chicken on each piece of dough; wrap dough around chicken and seal, pressing edges together tightly. Place seam side down on prepared baking sheet.

4. Bake 15 to 17 minutes or until light golden brown. Decorate with mustard and ketchup. Serve warm with additional mustard and ketchup for dipping.

Devilishly Deviled Eggs

Makes 12 halves

6 hard-cooked eggs, peeled
3 tablespoons mayonnaise
½ teaspoon Dijon mustard
¼ teaspoon salt
⅛ teaspoon white pepper

⅛ teaspoon chili powder
1 red bell pepper
1 green bell pepper
Fresh chives
24 black sesame seeds

1. Slice eggs in half lengthwise. Place yolks in medium bowl. Add mayonnaise, mustard, salt, white pepper and chili powder to yolks; mix well. Pipe or spoon filling into egg whites.

2. Cut 24 small triangles from red bell pepper and 12 small triangles from green bell pepper. Cut 24 (½- to 1-inch) pieces of chives. Make devil's face on egg yolk by adding red peppers for "horns", chives for "moustache" and green pepper for "goatee." Add two sesame seeds for "eyes." Cover; refrigerate 30 minutes before serving.

Campfire Hot Dogs

Makes 8 servings

Prep Time: 5 minutes   **Cook Time:** 10 minutes

½ pound ground beef
2 cups RAGÚ® Old World Style® Pasta Sauce
1 can (10¾ to 16 ounces) baked beans

8 frankfurters, cooked
8 frankfurter rolls

1. In 12-inch skillet, brown ground beef over medium-high heat; drain.

2. Stir in Pasta Sauce and beans. Bring to a boil over high heat. Reduce heat to low and simmer, stirring occasionally, 5 minutes.

3. To serve, arrange frankfurters in rolls and top with sauce mixture. Garnish, if desired, with Cheddar cheese.

Devilishly
Deviled Eggs

Chocolate Chip S'More Bites

Makes about 4 dozen s'mores

1 package (about 16 ounces) refrigerated
chocolate chip cookie dough
¾ cup semisweet chocolate chips

¼ cup plus 2 tablespoons whipping cream
½ cup marshmallow creme
½ cup sour cream

1. Preheat oven to 325°F. Spray 13×9-inch baking pan with nonstick cooking spray.

2. Press cookie dough into prepared pan, using damp hands to spread dough into even layer and cover bottom of pan. (Dough will be very thin.) Bake 20 minutes or until light golden brown and just set. Cool in pan on wire rack.

3. Meanwhile, place chocolate chips in medium bowl. Microwave whipping cream in small bowl on HIGH 1 minute. Pour over chocolate chips. Let stand 2 minutes; stir until smooth. Let stand 10 minutes or until thickened.

4. Combine marshmallow creme and sour cream in small bowl until smooth.

5. Cut bars into 1¼-inch squares with sharp knife. For each s'more, spread chocolate mixture on bottom of one square; spread marshmallow mixture on bottom of second square. Press together to form s'mores.

On a Stick

Banana Freezer Pops

Makes 8 servings

2 ripe medium bananas
1 can (6 ounces) frozen orange juice
    concentrate
¼ cup water

1 tablespoon honey
1 teaspoon vanilla
8 (3-ounce) paper or plastic cups
8 wooden sticks

1. Combine bananas, orange juice concentrate, water, honey and vanilla in food processor or blender; process until smooth.

2. Pour banana mixture evenly into cups. Cover top of each cup with small piece of foil. Insert wooden stick through center of foil into banana mixture.

3. Place cups on tray; freeze 3 hours or until firm. To serve, remove foil and paper cups.

Peppy Purple Pops: Omit honey and vanilla. Substitute grape juice concentrate for orange juice concentrate.

Caramel Corn Apple-Os

Makes 16 balls

7 cups popped popcorn
2¼ cups apple-cinnamon cereal rings
½ cup chopped dried apples or apricots
1 package (14 ounces) soft caramels

2 tablespoons butter
1 to 2 tablespoons water
16 cinnamon sticks (optional)
16 paper baking cups

Microwave Directions

1. Place 16 paper baking cups on baking sheet. Combine popcorn, cereal and dried apples in large bowl.

2. Place caramels, butter and water in large microwavable bowl. Microwave on HIGH 2½ to 3 minutes or until melted and smooth, stirring after each minute.

3. Pour caramel mixture over popcorn mixture; toss to coat. Let set until cool enough to handle.

4. Using damp hands, shape mixture into 16 balls. Gently insert cinnamon sticks. Place in paper baking cups on prepared baking sheet.

Creamy Strawberry-Orange Pops

Makes 6 servings

1 container (8 ounces) strawberry yogurt
¾ cup orange juice
2 teaspoons vanilla
2 cups frozen whole strawberries

2 teaspoons sugar
6 (7-ounce) paper cups
6 wooden sticks

1. Combine yogurt, orange juice and vanilla in blender or food processor; blend until smooth. Add strawberries and sugar; blend until smooth. Pour into cups, filling each about three-fourths full. Freeze 1 hour.

2. Insert wooden stick into center of each. Freeze completely. Peel cup off each pop to serve.

**Caramel Corn
Apple-Os**

Busy Bees

Makes about 24 pops

½ **baked and cooled 13×9-inch cake***
½ **cup plus 2 tablespoons frosting**
1 **package (14 to 16 ounces) yellow candy coating discs, divided**
24 **lollipop sticks**

Foam block
Black decorator frosting
Black string licorice, cut into ¾-inch lengths

*Prepare a cake from a mix according to package directions or use your favorite recipe. Cake must be cooled completely.

1. Line large baking sheet with waxed paper. Use hands to crumble cake into large bowl. (You should end up with fine crumbs and no large cake pieces remaining.)

2. Add frosting to cake crumbs; mix with hands until well blended. Shape mixture into 1½-inch balls (about 2 tablespoons cake mixture per ball); place on prepared baking sheet. Cover with plastic wrap; refrigerate at least 1 hour or freeze 10 minutes to firm.

3. Cut 24 yellow candy coating discs in half for wings; set aside. Cut small piece from each half to create flat edge.

4. When cake balls are firm, place remaining yellow candy coating discs in deep microwavable bowl. Melt according to package directions. Dip one lollipop stick about ½ inch into melted coating; insert stick into cake ball (no more than halfway through). Return cake pop to baking sheet in refrigerator to set. Repeat with remaining cake balls and sticks.

5. Working with one cake pop at a time, hold stick and dip cake ball into melted coating to cover completely, letting excess coating drip off. Rotate stick gently and/or tap stick on edge of bowl, if necessary, to remove excess coating. Place cake pop in foam block.

6. Pipe three stripes of black frosting around each cake pop. Dip toothpick in candy coating; place two dots of coating behind center stripe. Press reserved yellow disc halves, flat sides facing you, into coating for wings; hold in place until coating is set.

7. Pipe two dots of frosting at top of first stripe; attach two licorice pieces for antennae and hold in place until set. Pipe eyes and smile with black frosting.

Wild Watermelon Pops

Makes 4 pops

2 cups diced seedless watermelon (1-inch cubes)

2 tablespoons strawberry fruit spread

1 cup vanilla frozen yogurt

4 (5-ounce) paper or plastic cups or pop molds

4 teaspoons mini semisweet chocolate chips

4 pop sticks

1. Combine 1 cup watermelon and fruit spread in blender or food processor; blend until smooth. Add remaining 1 cup watermelon; blend until smooth and well combined. Add frozen yogurt, ½ cup at a time, blending until smooth after each addition.

2. Pour mixture into cups. Freeze 1 hour or until mixture just begins to harden.

3. Stir mixture in cups until smooth and slushy. Stir 1 teaspoon chocolate chips into each cup. Smooth top of mixture with back of spoon. Cover top of each cup with small piece of foil. Freeze 1 hour.

4. Insert sticks through center of foil. Freeze 4 hours or until firm.

5. To serve, remove foil and peel away paper cups or gently twist frozen pops out of plastic cups.

Tip: To use cone-shaped paper cups, line a baking sheet with regular-shaped 5-ounce paper cups, bottom sides up. Cut a small hole in the bottom of each regular-shaped paper cup. Place a cone-shaped cup, tip side down, in the hole to hold the pop in place.

Crushed Tortilla Corn Dogs

Makes 8 corn dogs

Prep Time: 20 minutes   **Start to Finish:** 30 minutes

2 cups vegetable oil
½ cup all-purpose flour
6 ORTEGA® Whole Grain Corn Taco Shells
1 cup prepared pancake mix
1 cup milk
1 egg

1 tablespoon ORTEGA® Taco Seasoning Mix
8 beef hot dogs
8 chopsticks or wooden skewers
½ cup ORTEGA® Thick & Chunky Salsa
¼ cup prepared yellow mustard

HEAT oil in medium saucepan over medium-high heat to 375°F. Line platter with paper towels. Place flour in shallow bowl or pie plate. Set aside.

PLACE taco shells in food processor and pulse until evenly ground. Transfer to another shallow bowl or pie plate. Add pancake mix, milk, egg and seasoning mix; mix well. Let stand 10 minutes.

THREAD hot dogs onto chopsticks. Coat hot dogs in flour, then coat evenly with batter.

LOWER hot dogs into hot oil carefully. Cook 4 to 5 minutes or until coating is golden brown. Remove by grasping chopstick "handle" with tongs. Drain on paper towels.

SERVE with salsa and mustard for dipping.

Tip: To crush taco shells without a food processor, place them in a resealable food storage bag and run a rolling pin over the shells until they're evenly crushed.

Chocolate-Dipped Caramel Apples

Makes 6 servings

1 package (14 ounces) caramels
1 tablespoon water
6 medium apples
6 wooden craft sticks

4 ounces milk or semisweet chocolate
confectionery coating, coarsely chopped
Assorted halloween sprinkles and decors

1. Line baking sheet with waxed paper. Unwrap caramels. Combine caramels and water in medium saucepan; cook over medium heat, stirring constantly, until caramels are melted.

2. Rinse and thoroughly dry apples; insert wooden sticks into stem ends. Dip apples, one at a time, into caramel mixture, coating completely. Remove excess caramel mixture by scraping apple bottom across rim of saucepan. Place on waxed paper. Refrigerate until caramel hardens.

3. Place confectionery coating in small saucepan. Cook over low heat, stirring frequently, until coating is melted. Dip apples halfway into coating. Return to waxed paper.

4. Decorate apples with sprinkles and decors as desired. Refrigerate until firm.

Pizza Dippin' Strips

Makes 16 strips

Prep Time: 10 minutes   **Cook Time:** 15 minutes

1 package (13.8 ounces) refrigerated pizza crust
15 thin slices pepperoni
1 cup shredded mozzarella cheese
(about 4 ounces)

1 jar (1 pound 8 ounces) RAGÚ® Old World Style Pasta Sauce or RAGÚ® Organic Pasta Sauce, heated

1. Preheat oven to 400°F.

2. Roll pizza crust into 12×9-inch rectangle on greased baking sheet. Fold edges over to make ¾-inch crust. Bake 7 minutes.

3. Evenly top pizza crust with pepperoni, then cheese. Bake an additional 8 minutes or until cheese is melted. Let stand 2 minutes.

4. Cut pizza in half lengthwise, then into 1½-inch strips. Serve with Pasta Sauce, heated, for dipping.

Grilled Cheese Kabobs

Makes 12 servings

8 thick slices whole wheat bread
3 thick slices sharp Cheddar cheese

3 thick slices Monterey Jack or Colby Jack cheese
2 tablespoons butter, melted

1. Cut each slice bread into 1-inch squares. Cut each slice cheese into 1-inch squares. Make small sandwiches with one square of bread and one square of each type of cheese. Top with second square of bread. Place sandwiches on the ends of short wooden skewers. Brush four sides of sandwiches with melted butter.

2. Heat nonstick grill pan over medium-high heat. Grill sandwich kabobs 30 seconds on each of four sides or until golden and cheese is slightly melted.

**Pizza
Dippin'
Strips**

Marshmallow Pops

Makes 20 marshmallow pops

Prep Time: 30 minutes   **Cooking Time:** 5 minutes   **Cooling Time:** 10 minutes

20 lollipop sticks (found at cake decorating or craft stores)
20 large marshmallows
1 cup (6 ounces) NESTLÉ® TOLL HOUSE® Premier White Morsels

1 cup (6 ounces) NESTLÉ® TOLL HOUSE® Milk Chocolate Morsels
Decorating icing
Assorted NESTLÉ® Candies and Chocolate*
NESTLÉ® RAISINETS®, NESTLÉ® SNO-CAPS®, WONKA® NERDS®, WONKA® TART 'N TINYS® and/or SweeTARTS® Gummy Bugs

LINE baking sheet with wax paper.

PUSH each lollipop stick halfway through a large marshmallow; set aside.

MELT white morsels according to package directions. Immediately dip *10* marshmallow lollipops lightly in the melted morsels for a thin coating. Set stick-side-up on prepared baking sheet.

MELT milk chocolate morsels according to package directions. Repeat dipping process as above with *remaining* marshmallows.

REFRIGERATE marshmallow lollipops for 10 minutes or until hardened. Use decorating icing as glue to decorate with assorted candies.

On a Stick

Corn Dogs

Makes 8 servings

Prep Time: 15 minutes   **Cook Time:** 20 minutes

8 hot dogs
8 wooden craft sticks
1 package (about 16 ounces) refrigerated
   grand-size corn biscuits

⅓ cup FRENCH'S® Classic Yellow® Mustard
8 slices American cheese, cut in half

1. Preheat oven to 350°F. Insert 1 wooden craft stick halfway into each hot dog; set aside.

2. Separate biscuits. On floured board, press or roll each biscuit into a 7×4-inch oval. Spread *2 teaspoons* mustard lengthwise down center of each biscuit. Top each with 2 pieces of cheese. Place hot dog in center of biscuit. Fold top of dough over end of hot dog. Fold sides towards center enclosing hot dog. Pinch edges to seal.

3. Place corn dogs, seam-side down, on greased baking sheet. Bake 20 to 25 minutes or until golden brown. Cool slightly before serving.

Tip: Corn dogs may be made without wooden craft sticks.

Cherry-Peach Pops

Makes 7 servings

⅓ cup peach or apricot nectar	1 carton (6 or 8 ounces) peach or cherry yogurt
1 teaspoon unflavored gelatin	1 carton (6 or 8 ounces) cherry yogurt
1 can (15 ounces) sliced peaches in light syrup, drained	7 (3-ounce) paper cups
	7 wooden craft sticks

1. Combine nectar and gelatin in small saucepan; let stand 5 minutes. Heat and stir over low heat just until gelatin dissolves.

2. Combine nectar mixture, peaches and yogurts in blender or food processor; blend until smooth.

3. Pour into cups, filling each about two-thirds full. Place in freezer; freeze 1 hour. Insert wooden stick into center of each cup. Freeze 3 hours.

4. Let stand at room temperature 10 minutes before serving. Tear away paper cups to serve.

Watermelon Kebabs

Makes 6 servings

18 (1-inch) cubes seedless watermelon	6 ounces (1-inch cubes) reduced-fat Cheddar cheese
6 ounces (1-inch cubes) fat-free turkey breast	6 (6-inch) bamboo skewers

Alternate cubes of watermelon between cubes of turkey and cheese threaded onto each skewer.

Favorite Recipe from *National Watermelon Promotion Board*

Cherry-Peach
Pops

Nutty Chocolate Banana Pops

Makes 8 servings

Prep Time: 20 minutes   **Freeze Time:** 2 hours

REYNOLDS® CUT-RITE® Wax Paper
4 ripe bananas
8 wooden sticks

CHOCOLATE DIP

REYNOLDS WRAP® Non-Stick Foil
1½ cups semi-sweet chocolate chips
2 tablespoons peanut butter
½ cup finely chopped nuts

CUT bananas crosswise in half. Insert wooden sticks in each half; set aside.

MICROWAVE chocolate chips and peanut butter in a medium microwave-safe bowl on HIGH power, 1 to 2 minutes, stirring every 30 seconds until chocolate is melted.

LINE counter with an 18-inch sheet of REYNOLDS® CUT-RITE® Wax Paper. Pour melted chocolate mixture on one end of wax paper and nuts on the opposite end.

ROLL banana pop in melted chocolate to coat evenly; immediately roll in chopped nuts. Place banana pops on a tray lined with wax paper. Place tray in freezer for 2 hours.

WRAP each banana pop in Reynolds Wrap Non-Stick Foil. Store in freezer.

Tiny Taffy Apples

Makes about 24 pops

½ **baked and cooled 13×9-inch cake***
½ **cup plus 2 tablespoons frosting**
 1 **package (14 to 16 ounces) peanut butter candy coating**
24 **lollipop sticks**

 2 **cups chopped peanuts**
24 **paper baking cups (optional)**

*Prepare a cake from a mix according to package directions or use your favorite recipe. Cake must be cooled completely.

1. Line large baking sheet with waxed paper. Use hands to crumble cake into large bowl. (You should end up with fine crumbs and no large cake pieces remaining.)

2. Add frosting to cake crumbs; mix with hands until well blended. Shape mixture into 1½-inch balls (about 2 tablespoons cake mixture per ball); place on prepared baking sheet. Cover with plastic wrap; refrigerate at least 1 hour or freeze 10 minutes to firm.

3. When cake balls are firm, place candy coating in deep microwavable bowl. Melt according to package directions. Dip one lollipop stick about ½ inch into melted coating; insert stick into cake ball (no more than halfway through). Return cake pop to baking sheet in refrigerator to set. Repeat with remaining cake balls and sticks.

4. Place peanuts in shallow bowl. Working with one cake pop at a time, hold stick and dip cake ball into melted coating to cover completely, letting excess coating drip off. Rotate stick gently and/or tap stick on edge of bowl, if necessary, to remove excess coating.

5. Immediately roll cake pop in peanuts to coat; press peanuts in gently to adhere to coating. Place cake pops in baking cups, if desired.

Easy PB 'n Chocolate Pretzels

Makes 28 servings

Prep Time: 5 minutes   **Cook Time:** 2 minutes   **Chill Time:** 15 minutes

1 cup semi-sweet chocolate chips
½ cup SKIPPY® Creamy Peanut Butter

1 bag (10 ounces) pretzel rods (about 28 pretzels)

Microwave chocolate chips with SKIPPY® Creamy Peanut Butter in medium microwave-safe bowl at HIGH, stirring occasionally, 1½ minutes or until melted and smooth. Dip one end of pretzels in peanut butter mixture, then arrange on waxed paper-lined baking sheets. Decorate, if desired, with colored sprinkles or nonpareils. Chill in refrigerator about 15 minutes or until set, OR at room temperature about 30 minutes.

Peachy Pops

Makes 8 pops

1 package (16 ounces) frozen sliced peaches, softened, but not completely thawed
2 containers (6 ounces each) peach or vanilla yogurt

¼ cup honey
8 (5-ounce) paper or plastic cups or pop molds
8 pop sticks
Assorted decorating sugars or sprinkles

1. Combine peaches, yogurt and honey in blender or food processor; blend until smooth. Pour mixture into cups. Cover top of each cup with small piece of foil. Freeze 2 hours.

2. Insert sticks through center of foil. Freeze 6 hours or until firm.

3. Remove foil and peel away paper cups or gently twist frozen pops out of plastic cups. Spread sugars on small plate; roll pops in sugar. Serve immediately or place in paper cups and return to freezer until ready to serve.

Easy PB 'n Chocolate Pretzels

Calzone-on-a-Stick

Makes 8 servings

Prep Time: 20 minutes   **Cook Time:** 15 minutes

8 wooden craft sticks
8 turkey or chicken sausage links (about
    1½ pounds), cooked
1 package (16.3 ounces) refrigerated grand-size
    biscuits

1 jar (1 pound 8 ounces) RAGÚ® Old World
    Style® Pasta Sauce
4 mozzarella cheese sticks, halved lengthwise

1. Preheat oven to 350°F. Insert craft stick halfway into each sausage; set aside.

2. Separate biscuits. On lightly floured surface, roll each biscuit into 7×4-inch oval. Place 2 tablespoons Pasta Sauce on long side of each oval. Top with sausage and ½ mozzarella stick. Fold dough over and pinch edges to seal. On greased baking sheet, arrange calzones seam-side down.

3. Bake 15 minutes or until golden. Serve with remaining Pasta Sauce, heated, for dipping.

Colorful Kabobs

Makes 10 kabobs

30 cocktail-size smoked sausages
10 to 20 cherry or grape tomatoes
10 to 20 large pimiento-stuffed green olives

2 yellow bell peppers, cut into 1-inch squares
¼ cup (½ stick) butter, melted
Lemon juice (optional)

1. Preheat oven to 450°F. Thread 3 sausages onto 8-inch wooden skewer,* alternating with tomatoes, olives and bell peppers. Repeat on remaining nine skewers.

2. Place skewers on rack in shallow baking pan. Brush with melted butter and drizzle with lemon juice, if desired. Bake 4 to 6 minutes or until heated through.

Soak skewers in water 20 minutes before using to prevent them from burning.

**Calzone-
on-a-Stick**

Magic Rainbow Pops

Makes about 6 pops

1 envelope (¼ ounce) unflavored gelatin
¼ cup cold water
½ cup boiling water
1 container (6 ounces) raspberry or strawberry yogurt

1 container (6 ounces) lemon or orange yogurt
1 can (8¼ ounces) apricots or peaches with juice
Pop molds with lids

1. Combine gelatin and cold water in 2-cup glass measuring cup. Let stand 5 minutes to soften. Add boiling water. Stir until gelatin is completely dissolved. Cool.

2. For first layer, combine raspberry yogurt and ¼ cup gelatin mixture in small bowl; stir until completely blended. Fill each pop mold about one third full with raspberry mixture.* Freeze 30 to 60 minutes or until set.

3. For second layer, combine lemon yogurt and ¼ cup gelatin mixture in small bowl; stir until completely blended. Pour lemon mixture over raspberry layer in each mold.* Freeze 30 to 60 minutes or until set.

4. For third layer, combine apricots with juice and remaining ¼ cup gelatin mixture in blender or food processor; blend until smooth. Pour mixture over lemon layer in each mold.* Cover with lids. Freeze 2 to 5 hours or until firm.**

5. To remove pops from molds, place bottoms of pops under warm running water until loosened. Press firmly on bottoms to release. (Do not twist or pull lids.)

Pour any extra mixture into small paper cups. Freeze as directed in tip.
**If you are not using pop molds with lids, cover each pop with small piece of foil and insert sticks through center of foil.*

Tip: Three-ounce paper or plastic cups can be used in place of the molds.
Make the layers as directed or put a single flavor in each cup and cover each
cup with small piece of foil and freeze 1 hour before inserting sticks. Freeze until firm.
To serve, remove foil and peel away paper cups or gently twist frozen pops out of plastic cups.

Index

Index

Index

Index

Acknowledgments

The publisher would like to thank the companies and organizations listed below for the use of their recipes and photographs in this publication.

ACH Food Company
Campbell Soup Company
Cream of Wheat® Cereal
The Hershey Company
Hormel Foods, The Makers of Skippy® Peanut Butter
National Watermelon Promotion Board
Nestlé USA
Ortega®, A division of B&G Foods, Inc.
The Quaker® Oatmeal Kitchens
Reckitt Benckiser LLC.
Recipes courtesy of the Reynolds Kitchens
Unilever

Metric Conversion Chart

VOLUME MEASUREMENTS (dry)

$\frac{1}{8}$ teaspoon = 0.5 mL
$\frac{1}{4}$ teaspoon = 1 mL
$\frac{1}{2}$ teaspoon = 2 mL
$\frac{3}{4}$ teaspoon = 4 mL
1 teaspoon = 5 mL
1 tablespoon = 15 mL
2 tablespoons = 30 mL
$\frac{1}{4}$ cup = 60 mL
$\frac{1}{3}$ cup = 75 mL
$\frac{1}{2}$ cup = 125 mL
$\frac{2}{3}$ cup = 150 mL
$\frac{3}{4}$ cup = 175 mL
1 cup = 250 mL
2 cups = 1 pint = 500 mL
3 cups = 750 mL
4 cups = 1 quart = 1 L

VOLUME MEASUREMENTS (fluid)

1 fluid ounce (2 tablespoons) = 30 mL
4 fluid ounces ($\frac{1}{2}$ cup) = 125 mL
8 fluid ounces (1 cup) = 250 mL
12 fluid ounces (1$\frac{1}{2}$ cups) = 375 mL
16 fluid ounces (2 cups) = 500 mL

WEIGHTS (mass)

$\frac{1}{2}$ ounce = 15 g
1 ounce = 30 g
3 ounces = 90 g
4 ounces = 120 g
8 ounces = 225 g
10 ounces = 285 g
12 ounces = 360 g
16 ounces = 1 pound = 450 g

DIMENSIONS

$\frac{1}{16}$ inch = 2 mm
$\frac{1}{8}$ inch = 3 mm
$\frac{1}{4}$ inch = 6 mm
$\frac{1}{2}$ inch = 1.5 cm
$\frac{3}{4}$ inch = 2 cm
1 inch = 2.5 cm

OVEN TEMPERATURES

250°F = 120°C
275°F = 140°C
300°F = 150°C
325°F = 160°C
350°F = 180°C
375°F = 190°C
400°F = 200°C
425°F = 220°C
450°F = 230°C

BAKING PAN AND DISH EQUIVALENTS

Utensil	Size in Inches	Size in Centimeters	Volume	Metric Volume
Baking or Cake Pan (square or rectangular)	8×8×2	20×20×5	8 cups	2 L
	9×9×2	23×23×5	10 cups	2.5 L
	13×9×2	33×23×5	12 cups	3 L
Loaf Pan	8$\frac{1}{2}$×4$\frac{1}{2}$×2$\frac{1}{2}$	21×11×6	6 cups	1.5 L
	9×9×3	23×13×7	8 cups	2 L
Round Layer Cake Pan	8×1$\frac{1}{2}$	20×4	4 cups	1 L
	9×1$\frac{1}{2}$	23×4	5 cups	1.25 L
Pie Plate	8×1$\frac{1}{2}$	20×4	4 cups	1 L
	9×1$\frac{1}{2}$	23×4	5 cups	1.25 L
Baking Dish or Casserole			1 quart/4 cups	1 L
			1$\frac{1}{2}$ quart/6 cups	1.5 L
			2 quart/8 cups	2 L
			3 quart/12 cups	3 L